THE FOX JUMPS OVER
THE PARSON'S GATE

Grolier Educational Corporation

THE Huntsman blows his horn in the morn,
When folks goes hunting, oh!
When folks goes hunting, oh!
When folks goes hunting, oh!
The Huntsman blows his horn in the morn,
When folks goes hunting, oh!

The Fox jumps over the Parson's gate,
And the Hounds all after him go,
And the Hounds all after him go,
And the Hounds all after him go.

But all my fancy dwells on Nancy,
So I'll cry, Tally-ho!
So I'll cry, Tally-ho!

Now the PARSON had a pair to wed
    As the Hounds came full in view;
He tossed his surplice over his head,
    And bid them all adieu!

But all my fancy dwelt on NANCY,
    So he cried, TALLY-HO!
    So he cried, TALLY-HO!

Oh! never despise the soldier-lad
　　Though his station be but low,
　　Though his station be but low,
　　Though his station be but low.

But all my fancy dwells on Nancy,
　　So I'll cry, Tally-ho!

Then pass around the jug, my boys;
    For we must homewards go,
    For we must homewards go,
    For we must homewards go.
And if you ask me of this song
    The reason for to show,
    I don't exactly know – ow – ow,
    I don't exactly know.

But all my fancy dwells on Nancy,
So I'll sing, Tally-ho!
So I'll sing, Tally-ho!
But all my fancy dwells on Nancy,
So I'll sing, TALLY-HO!

Distributed under exclusive licence in North America by Grolier
Educational Corporation.

Copyright © 1988 New Orchard Editions.

ISBN 0-7172-9022-0

Printed in Portugal